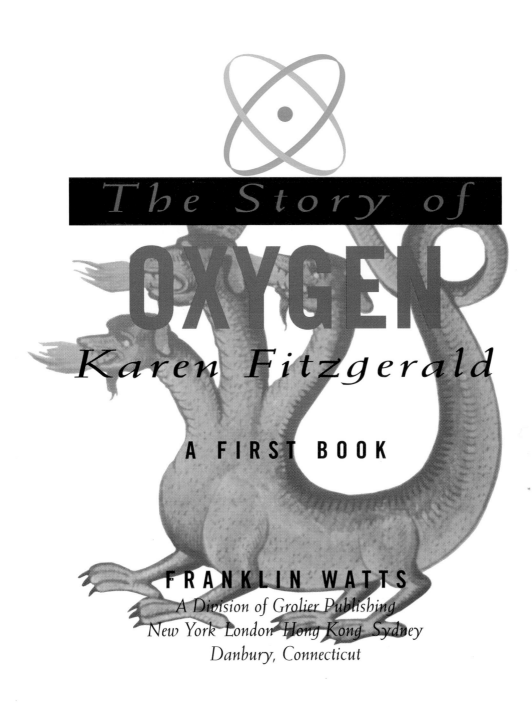

The Story of

OXYGEN

Karen Fitzgerald

A FIRST BOOK

FRANKLIN WATTS
A Division of Grolier Publishing
New York London Hong Kong Sydney
Danbury, Connecticut

To Ross

Chemical consultant: Geoffrey Buckwalter, Ph.D.
Cover and interior design by Robin Hessel Hoffmann
Photographs copyright ©: UPI/Bettmann: p. 6; The Bettmann Archive: pp. 14,
22, 47; Photo Researchers: pp. 8 (Biophoto Associates/SS), 26 (Charles D. Win-
ters), 32 (Andrew McClenaghan/SPL), 34, 53 (both photos by Ken Eward/SS),
44 (Tom Myers), 49 (Ken Eward/BioGrafx-SS), 50 (Herbert Schwind/Okapia),
54 (NASA/SS); North Wind Picture Archives: pp. 10, 23; Comstock: p. 13
(Laura Elliot); Archive Photos: pp. 16, 30; Edgar Fahs Smith Collection,
Department of Special Collections, Van Pelt-Dietrich Library,
University of Pennsylvania: pp. 18, 20.

Library of Congress Cataloging-in-Publication Data

Fitzgerald, Karen.
        The story of oxygen / by Karen Fitzgerald.
    p.   cm.—(A first book)
    Includes bibliographical references (p.   ) and index.
    Summary: Explores the history of the chemical element oxygen and explains
its chemistry, how it works in the body, and its importance in our lives.
    ISBN 0-531-20225-9
    1. Oxygen—Juvenile literature. [1. Oxygen.] I. Title. II. Series.
QD181.01f55   1996   96-6202
546'.721—dc20   CIP AC

Contents

Chapter 1
THE FIRE-BREATHING DRAGON
5

Chapter 2
DISCOVERING OXYGEN
9

Chapter 3
THE SECRET OF FIRE
25

Chapter 4
THE DRAGON OF THE AIR
31

Chapter 5
THE FIRE OF LIFE
46

GLOSSARY
56

SOURCES
60

INDEX
61

Chapter 1

THE FIRE-BREATHING DRAGON

Millions of years ago, people were afraid of fire. They wouldn't go near it because it was so different from anything else in the world. The roaring flames must have seemed like a horrifying, wild monster rapidly covering the land. It destroyed large areas of forests, leaving behind only black stumps. No wonder people and animals ran away!

Early humans didn't know it, but the secret of the monster was a wondrous substance called oxygen. If they had known this invisible gas was in the air keeping them alive, they might not have been so frightened of fire. But back then, they had no idea that oxygen existed. They didn't even know there was such a thing as air.

To early people, fire must have seemed like a scary monster.

Although fire scared them, its mysterious beauty must have attracted early people. Perhaps it was the light and warmth of the dancing flames that eventually drew people near. At some point, they overcame their fear and learned to make fire for themselves. It helped them stay warm and gave them light to see in the darkness. They soon discovered many other ways that fire could help them.

Imagine cave people gathering around fires at night, spellbound by the lively flames. They must have wondered: What can the brilliant, orange glow possibly be? You may have wondered that yourself at a campfire or in front of a fireplace.

Even today, fire is like nothing else in the world. It isn't solid, but it isn't liquid either. It is more like air than anything, but it is still very different from air. Fire jumps and flickers as if it has a life of its own.

The mystery of fire was not solved until hundreds of thousands of years after people learned to control it. One reason it took so long is that oxygen is invisible and has no smell, taste, or sound. It seems unbelievable that something so quiet and gentle could be responsible for something as wild as fire. But it is. Once scientists discovered oxygen, they began to see just how truly amazing it is.

They learned that oxygen makes a slow fire in us, too. With every breath, we take oxygen into our lungs, where it passes into our blood. From there it travels to all the cells in our bodies and gives them the energy they need to keep us alive. A breath of oxygen is a jolt of life.

Blood carries oxygen to all the cells of our bodies.

Oxygen is really like a lovable creature that wants to bond with everything it meets. Because of that, it is part of most of what we see around us. Without oxygen, people, animals, and plants would not exist.

So you see, oxygen seemed as scary as a fire-breathing dragon at first, but it turned out to be full of wonderful surprises. If you read on, you will get to know all about this fire-breathing dragon. You will learn the secrets of fire and breath and all the ways oxygen has affected our lives. You will see that it has given us a lot to be thankful for. But you will also find that it can sometimes be very harmful.

By the time you finish this book, you will know much of what scientists know about oxygen and the role it plays in the world. This is the story of oxygen.

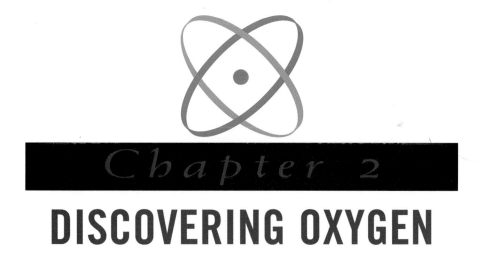

Chapter 2

DISCOVERING OXYGEN

People were very close to the fire-breathing dragon for ages, but they didn't know it. Oxygen was a constant companion, flowing into their nostrils and mouths, keeping them alive.

The first visible clue that oxygen existed was fire started by lightning. People gradually came closer, until finally, some brave person probably carried away a burning branch and made a fire with it.

Perhaps early humans kept a small fire going all the time so that they could make a fire whenever they wanted to. Once they realized it could keep them warm and help them see at night, they must have known it would be very hard to live without. It could keep wild animals away, too.

Fire became very important to early humans.

Later, people learned to make a fire by rubbing sticks together until they were very hot. When the sticks got so hot that smoke appeared, fire came to life. Eventually people found that fire could cook meat, making it last longer and taste more delicious. Fire could also heat clay from the ground to make pots and dishes.

Then they discovered something truly extraordinary. If certain kinds of rocky material from the ground were heated to a high temperature, shiny liquids would drip out. When the liquid cooled, it became so hard it could be used for tools and weapons.

The shiny materials were metals, including copper, lead, iron, and silver. They came from rocky material called ore. Heating a green ore produced copper, for instance, and a red ore produced lead.

So you see, fire was necessary for the development of civilization. It helped bring people together for warmth and light, and it gave them tools for an easier life. Because of fire, they did not have to worry so much about surviving. They had more time to develop such things as art and writing. As they progressed, people had more and more time to think about the world.

THE DISCOVERY OF AIR

People began to notice that some of the things around them were solid like earth, and others were liquid like water. Fire, of course, was in a class by itself. About 450 B.C., a Greek named Empedocles discovered another kind of substance. It was air. He noticed that when he lowered a container, upside-down, into water, the water would not go into the container. Something was taking up space inside.

Empedocles realized it must be some kind of invisible substance. You see, when he made a small hole in the bottom of the container, the water would enter the container's main opening. The invisible substance was able to escape out of the hole, leaving room for the water. You can see this for yourself with a paper cup.

Air was obviously very different from earth, water, or fire. Empedocles decided that these four substances are basic forms of *matter*, which is anything that takes up space. He believed that these four basic substances, or *elements*, combine to create all the things on earth.

The idea of the four elements caught on quickly because it seemed to explain what happens when wood burns. The wood appears to break down into more basic substances, and they look a lot like earth, air, fire, and water. Fire seems to flow out of the wood. Smoke, rising from the wood and fading into the air, seems to be a kind of air. Beads of water appear to ooze out of the burning wood. And the ashes that remain look like earth. Since there was no way to test the idea of the four elements back then, it made a lot of sense to people for almost 2,000 years.

But eventually people called alchemists began experimenting with many different substances. They were looking for a way to change lead and other metals into gold.

No one ever found a way to make gold, but the alchemists did discover a lot about how substances react with one another. When some substances were mixed, a chemical reaction took place. They didn't just mix together like the ingredients in a cookie recipe, but rather transformed into a completely new substance. For instance,

To followers of the Greeks, a burning log appeared to break down into its elements—earth, air, fire, and water.

*Alchemists used symbols such as dragons
to represent chemical processes.*

certain liquids called *acids*, would dissolve metal, leaving
behind a powdery substance.

Fire often played a big part in chemical reactions.
When lead and other metals were heated so hot that they

were practically on fire, a powdery, earthlike substance appeared in place of the metal. Iron would turn into rust. The alchemists called rust the *earth* of iron.

FIRE AND AIR

The Chinese began studying alchemy hundreds of years B.C. According to some people, the first person to discover the secret of the fire-breathing dragon was a Chinese man named Mao-Khóa, who lived in the eighth century A.D.

Mao-Khóa believed that air is made of two parts, which he called *yang* and *yin*. He thought of yang as complete air and yin as incomplete air. So Mao-Khóa realized that air is made of two invisible gases. European chemists did not discover this until a thousand years later, when yin was named *oxygen* and yang was named *nitrogen*.

When charcoal or light metals burn in air, Mao-Khóa said, they combine with yin from the air. Yin is being removed from the surrounding air, making it more perfect. He also said that yin could be found as part of certain ores.

If this story is true, then Mao-Khóa knew that the secret of fire is oxygen. Today we know that fire is not a kind of matter at all, but a chemical reaction in which oxygen combines with the burning material. When charcoal burns, it links up with oxygen to form a new substance. Rather than destroying materials, fire brings them together!

Unfortunately, Europeans did not know about Mao-Khóa's work. They continued to believe for hundreds of

Leonardo da Vinci noticed that fire consumes
the part of the air that we breathe.

years that fire was an element. In the fifteenth century, the great Italian artist and scientist Leonardo da Vinci came close to Mao-Khóa's discovery. He noticed that as a flame burns, it sucks in a portion of the surrounding air. But he did not realize that this component of air combines with the burning material.

Da Vinci, who studied the human body, also discovered that the same part of air is taken into the body during breathing. He wrote, "Where flame cannot live, no animal that draws breath can live."

Da Vinci came to the conclusion that air is not an element, since it is composed of different parts. As time went on, more and more people began to doubt the four-element theory. It was not long before European scientists realized that fire is not an element, nor earth, since it contains more than one substance.

In the 1600s, an English doctor named John Mayow proved by a simple test that fire uses up a part of the air. He lit a candle standing in a pool of water and turned a bottle upside down over the candle. Most of the candle was above the water, and the bottle enclosed it and the surrounding air over the water. As the candle burned, the water rose up the side of the bottle! The flame was removing something from the air, and the water was replacing it. When the flame went out, the water stopped rising.

Mayow guessed that fire is caused by particles in the air colliding with particles in the flame. This, he thought, destroys the air particles and produces many tiny sparks that together create the flame.

Then Mayow tried putting a mouse instead of a candle in the bottle. As with the flame, the water rose up the side of the bottle. And even though the mouse remained above water, after awhile it began to suffocate.

Like Da Vinci, Mayow realized that animals breathe in the same part of air that fire uses. Mayow knew that animals absorb it into their blood in the lungs, and that it turns blood red. He also discovered another interesting thing

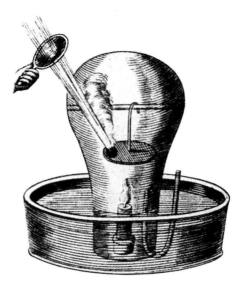

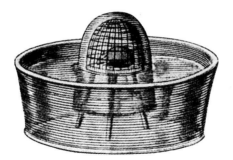

John Mayow's experiments included burning a candle in a bottle of air over water (top). He ignited the candle and other materials with the help of a magnifying glass. He also put a mouse in a similar setup to see whether it used up air as it breathed (bottom). In both cases, the water level rose.

having to do with air: the "earths" that were produced by heating metals weighed more than the metal. He guessed that the extra weight came from something in the air.

A WRONG TURN

After a few early scientists came so close to solving the mystery of fire, chemists in the 1700s somehow went off track. These chemists got the idea that a material on fire gives off something, rather than takes something from the air. They called this invisible substance *phlogiston*.

It seems they, like so many before them, were fooled by burning wood. If you watch a fire, you will see that it is a lot easier to imagine something escaping from the wood than something being added to it. Also, the ashes always weigh much less than the original piece of wood. Later, you will find that there is a good reason for that, but it has nothing to do with phlogiston.

Even though their explanation of fire was backwards, eighteenth-century chemists made many valuable discoveries about air. To their surprise, they found that there were many different kinds of air.

It all started with an English physiologist named Stephen Hales. He discovered that many materials give off "air" when they are heated strongly with fire. And he found a clever way to capture the air in a bottle.

The air was sent in a tube through a tub of water and up into an upside-down bottle filled with water. The air

Stephen Hales found a way to capture the air given off by burning substances.

from the heated materials would bubble out of the tube and up through the water. As the bubbles collected at the top, they would push the water level in the bottle down.

Hales tried cooking the red earth of lead to see if any air was given off. He was amazed at the enormous amount of air he collected. As it cooked, the earth was transformed into lead metal. Since the earth weighed more than the lead, Hales guessed that the air might account for the extra weight. He thought that air somehow became held in place, or fixed, in solid materials in such a way that it took up much less space.

Hales also found that materials from plants and dead animals gave off great amounts of air when they were heated. He didn't realize it, but this air was different from the air given off by lead's earth. Since they were both invisible, he assumed they were the same as the air around him.

In 1756 a Scottish chemist named Joseph Black finally began to notice that some "airs" were different from normal air. For instance, a flame would not light in the air given off by burning charcoal. And when he bubbled this air through a certain liquid chemical, the clear liquid turned a milky white. That didn't happen with normal air.

Black called this strange new air *fixed air* because he, like Hales, thought it was being held in place in the charcoal. It was the same air Hales had collected from plant and animal materials. Today chemists call it *carbon dioxide*.

Other chemists were very surprised by Black's findings, and many of them began investigating airs. In 1766 Henry Cavendish discovered another kind of air. It was given off when an acid dissolved a metal. This air could catch fire and quickly burn until it was gone. He called it *inflammable air*, which means air that burns easily. Today we know it as *hydrogen*.

At the time, many chemists thought fixed air and inflammable air were simply air with different particles added. But some were beginning to see that they are actually distinct from air. Today we know that they are not air at all, but substances called *gases*.

Two chemists working separately in the early 1770s discovered yet another gas. They recognized that it was different from anything they'd seen before because when they put a flame in it, the flame burned much more brightly. Carl Wilhelm Scheele, a Swedish chemist, said the

Carl Scheele became interested in chemistry during his work in a pharmacy, beginning when he was fourteen years old.

flame grew so much that it dazzled his eyes, so he called the new gas *fire air*. Of course, this gas was oxygen. He realized that air is made of oxygen and what he called *foul air*, which is nitrogen.

Joseph Priestley, an English chemist, discovered oxygen in 1774, about two years after Scheele. But because Priestley was the first to announce it in print, many people gave him credit for it. He discovered it by first heating the metal *mercury* in air until it turned into its red, powdery

Joseph Priestley was surprised by how light and easy his breathing felt when he breathed oxygen.

earth. Then he pointed a giant magnifying glass at the red earth to focus the heat of the sun on it. The red powder did not burn, but was roasted very hot, and it gave off a great deal of what Priestley called "air."

He found that he could generate the same gas using the earth of lead instead of mercury. Since he had made both red powders by heating metals in air, he began to suspect that the oxygen had come from the atmosphere.

He also wondered if his discovery might be the thing in air that keeps people and animals alive. So he tried breathing the oxygen. His chest felt lighter, and breathing became easier. You might say he felt more alive, just as the flame burned more brightly. Because of this, he thought the gas must be a pure kind of air. He wrote that it was "about five or six times as good as common air."

So people had finally recognized that oxygen existed, and it was right in front of their noses (and inside them, too) all those years! Even though many of them still considered it purified air, scientists recognized it as a substance with unique qualities, or *properties*. They were able to collect and identify oxygen by doing some simple tests.

Oxygen's most important property was the way it encouraged things to burn. But scientists were still confused about how it did that. It would be a few more years before they would have a true picture of the fire-breathing dragon.

Chapter 3

THE SECRET OF FIRE

Scheele and Priestley, who discovered oxygen, thought they knew exactly why fire burns more brightly in oxygen than in air. It sounds funny to us now, but they thought oxygen could absorb a lot of phlogiston. Yes, that's the invisible substance they believed flowed out of a burning material. They thought a flame could not burn in carbon dioxide and nitrogen because these "airs" were already full of phlogiston and would not take any more. And that's what most chemists believed at the time.

But if that was true, one thing didn't make sense. Why did some substances gain weight when they were burned, or heated strongly? Wood and other materials from plants and animals lost weight, but metals, for instance, gained weight.

When the metal mercury is heated in air, a red "earth"
is produced that weighs more than the mercury.

If phlogiston was flowing from metals as they roasted, why didn't they lose weight? In 1772 one chemist explained it by saying that phlogiston in metals buoys them up in the same way an inner tube buoys up a swimmer. As a result, the metal weighs more after it burns, when the phlogiston escapes into the air. Others said that perhaps phlogiston had negative weight!

When Antoine Lavoisier, a French chemist, heard these explanations, he knew they were ridiculous. He had already done his own experiments with fire and had concluded that the gain in weight of metals after burning must come from the air. Lavoisier believed that the air was chemically combining with the solids.

But Lavoisier did not know what kind of air it was. Soon after he heard about the discovery of fire air in 1774, Lavoisier realized that it was the air he was seeking and that it is the key to combustion.

Lavoisier also figured out how much oxygen the air contains. He mixed oxygen with different amounts of nitrogen until he found the combination that supported a flame the same size as one lit in regular air. From that test, he figured that a fifth of air is oxygen and about four-fifths is nitrogen.

HYDROGEN AND WATER

Lavoisier continued to do experiments with combustion so that he could understand it better. He was particularly interested in the burning of inflammable air, or hydrogen. It seemed very mysterious because when it burned in a bottle, the hydrogen and some of the oxygen inside seemed to disappear into thin air. As far as he could see, no other substance took their places. Shouldn't hydrogen combine with oxygen to form something else, as metals did?

About the same time, Priestley was doing his own experiments with hydrogen and oxygen. After the two gases reacted, he noticed tiny drops of moisture on the sides of the bottle, and he told Cavendish about them.

Cavendish decided to try the experiment himself to see if he got the drops too. Sure enough, he saw drops, and when he tested them, he found that they were water. He realized that the water must have come from the reaction. But like most other chemists of the time, Cavendish believed that hydrogen released phlogiston as it burned. So he assumed that hydrogen was made of water and phlogiston.

When Lavoisier heard about Cavendish's findings, he came to a very different conclusion. Lavoisier realized that water is not an element at all, but a *compound* made of oxygen and hydrogen. When hydrogen burns, it combines with oxygen to form a more complex substance.

Lavoisier was then certain that he had solved the mystery of fire. He could see that fire is the result of oxygen combining with another substance. When charcoal burns, oxygen from the air is sucked in to combine with the charcoal, which chemists call carbon. The result is a compound—the invisible gas carbon dioxide.

The escape of carbon dioxide into the air from a burning substance confused eighteenth-century chemists into thinking that fire is the release of phlogiston. Wood, which is made of mostly carbon, also gives off carbon dioxide when it burns, leaving behind ashes weighing much less than the original wood.

THE NEW ELEMENTS

In 1786, Lavoisier announced that there was no such thing as phlogiston. It took many years to convince other chemists of this, but gradually they realized he was right. Strangely enough, Priestley and Scheele never did. They both died still believing in phlogiston. So they never knew the important role oxygen plays in fire.

Lavoisier was the person who named oxygen. The name oxygen comes from Greek words for "acid maker." He had noticed that when many substances combine with oxygen, they become acidic. So he thought oxygen was responsible for acidity. He was wrong about that.

But he was right about fire—and water. Oxygen and hydrogen are elements, not water. This was the blow that finally overthrew the four-element theory. Lavoisier listed many other substances he thought might be elements because they had not been broken down into anything simpler. Some were metals, such as gold, silver, lead, and iron.

The "earths" of metals, such as lead, he realized, are compounds of oxygen and the metal. When metals are heated strongly, a slow combustion takes place. So in reality oxygen is the common element in the old four elements. It forms the bulk of our world.

Chemists soon began to discover more and more elements. Over the next 200 years, they found 92 elements in nature plus some that were generated artificially in the laboratory.

Antoine Lavoisier gave oxygen its name
and recognized that it is an element.

They started naming compounds according to the elements they contain. The earth of lead became lead oxide because it contains lead and oxygen. Likewise, the earth of mercury became mercuric oxide.

So you see, solving the mystery of fire helped set scientists on the road to modern chemistry. Chemists would discover many amazing things about the new elements, including oxygen. In fact, the fire-breathing dragon would play a starring role in the new chemistry.

Chapter 4

THE DRAGON
OF THE AIR

As Lavoisier's revolutionary ideas took over, chemists all over Europe began investigating the new elements and their compounds. It was an exciting time. Many chemists were fascinated by the strange new gases, including oxygen. Imagine discovering that there is a whole zoo of invisible creatures in the air around you that you never knew existed before.

If you were at all curious, you would want to know how these creatures behave and how they are different from one another. You might even try to visualize them— to imagine what they are made of. The gases were invisible, but the chemists knew they must contain something too small to see.

If it is cooled to -297°F (-183°C), oxygen becomes visible as a liquid. It freezes solid at -360°F (-218°C).

Back then, chemists knew very little about air. They knew it contained nitrogen, oxygen, and evaporated water. But they did not know whether the gases were chemically combined in a compound or just mixed together like fruit juices in punch.

One scientist who got to know air very well was John Dalton. In the hopes of finding a way to predict the weather, he studied the amount of water vapor in different parts of the atmosphere. Water vapor is just evaporated water, and it is an invisible gas, like oxygen. Dalton found that the air sometimes contains more water vapor, such as just before it rains.

Because the amount of water vapor varies, he realized that the vapor does not combine chemically with the air. You see, chemists had noticed that the elements in each compound always combine in the same proportions. For instance, whenever water forms, the oxygen used always weighs eight times as much as the hydrogen.

So Dalton guessed that particles of water vapor in the air simply spread through the spaces between air particles, rather than attaching to the particles. That is why air could hold different amounts of water vapor. Dalton realized that the particles of nitrogen and oxygen mix together in the same way, without attaching, or combining chemically.

Dalton thought more and more about the particles in these gases and in compounds. He concluded that every substance is made of zillions of particles called *atoms* that are too tiny to see. The atoms in each element, he guessed, are different from the atoms of any other element. For one thing, the weight of each atom varies from element to element.

He imagined that when a compound forms, the atoms of different elements gather together in little groups. For every compound, these groups, called *molecules*, always contain the same number of atoms from each element. That explained why the proportions of elements were always the same.

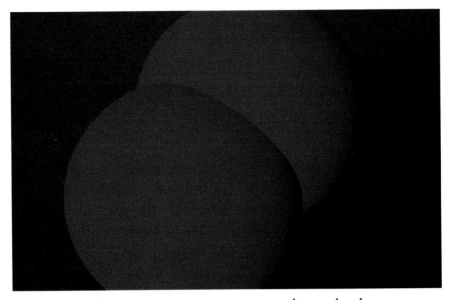

In the air, oxygen atoms are paired in molecules.

After awhile, other chemists realized that Dalton was right. They began representing compounds by the atoms in their molecules. Each element was given a symbol; oxygen became O and hydrogen became H. Since every molecule of water contains two atoms of hydrogen and one atom of oxygen, the symbol for water became H_2O. The symbol for carbon dioxide became CO_2.

Some gaseous elements, including oxygen, contain molecules of paired atoms. So the formula for oxygen gas is O_2. Air does not have a chemical symbol because it is a mixture, but it is made up of O_2, N_2, CO_2, H_2O, and very small amounts of other gases.

CHEMICAL LOVE

Soon after Lavoisier's discoveries, chemists found that they could separate water into hydrogen and oxygen by running electricity through it. As if by magic, the gases bubbled up out of the water. The chemists noticed something very curious about this process: hydrogen gas always rose out of the water at the negative wire of the battery, and oxygen gas rose near the positive wire.

Electricity had only recently been discovered, and scientists didn't know how it worked, but they imagined that it flowed from the negative wire to the positive wire. Electricity itself was negatively charged, they theorized, and so was attracted to the positively charged wire, much like opposite poles of a magnet attract each other.

So chemists began to wonder whether oxygen had a negative electrical charge and whether hydrogen had a positive electrical charge. As they separated other compounds with electricity, they saw that in every case, some elements gathered at the positive wire and others at the negative wire. It became clear that atoms bond together because of an electrical attraction for one another.

Oxygen always appeared at the positive wire, no matter which other elements were present. That was very unusual. Hydrogen, for instance, appeared at the negative wire when it was with oxygen, but appeared at the positive wire when it was with other elements.

Chemists began arranging the elements according to how electrically negative, or *electronegative*, they are. Oxygen, it turned out, was more electronegative than any other element discovered at that time. This was one of the first properties, or chemical characteristics, that chemists learned about oxygen.

You've probably heard that opposites attract. Well, it's certainly true with atoms. The greater the difference in the electronegativity of two atoms, the greater the attraction between them. Since oxygen is so extremely negative, it is very attracted to other atoms. It loves to bond with just about any element.

In fact, oxygen bonds with more elements than any other element does. Oxygen bonding is so prevalent in the world that chemists in the 1800s began using the term *oxidize* for it. When rust forms, for instance, iron is being oxidized; it is bonding with oxygen.

FAMILY BONDS

By the end of the 1800s, scientists had discovered that electricity is made of small particles called *electrons*. Each tiny electron has a negative electrical charge. Electrons come from the inside of an atom, and they move around its center, which is called the *nucleus*. The nucleus contains *protons*, positively charged particles that attract the electrons, holding them in place a distance away from the nucleus.

These electrons and protons gave chemists the answer to how elements differ from one another. Each element has a different number of electrons and protons. A hydrogen atom is the simplest of all the elements. It has one proton in its nucleus, surrounded by one electron. The oxygen atom has eight protons and eight electrons.

Gradually, chemists began to discover why oxygen is attracted to other elements. It is seeking atoms that are willing to share electrons with it. Two of its electrons are close to the nucleus, and the remaining six are further away. These six electrons aren't happy unless they have two more electrons to complete their family.

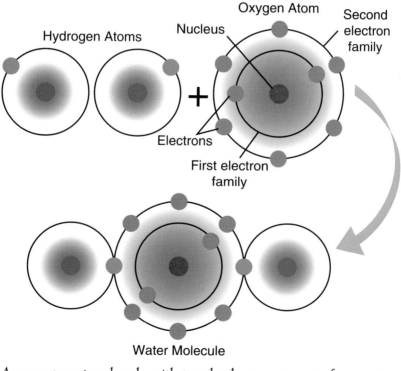

An oxygen atom bonds with two hydrogen atoms to form water.

Hydrogen is a favorite companion of oxygen because two hydrogen atoms gladly share their single electrons with an oxygen atom. It seems that these electrons would rather be part of a big happy family of eight.

Carbon, with six electrons, has four electrons in its outer family. One carbon atom can satisfy two oxygen atoms with these four electrons. That's why carbon dioxide forms. Carbon donates its electrons to oxygen and becomes positively charged. With extra electrons, the oxygen atoms become negatively charged. The electrical attractions between the carbon and oxygen atoms hold the carbon dioxide molecule together.

When bonding with hydrogen, carbon accepts rather than donates four electrons (from four hydrogen atoms) to make a complete outer family of eight. That's because it is more electronegative than hydrogen; carbon becomes negatively charged and hydrogen positively charged.

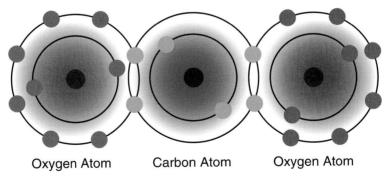

Oxygen Atom   Carbon Atom   Oxygen Atom

A carbon atom has four electrons in its outer family,
so it can satisfy two oxygen atoms.

Any time an atom donates electrons to another atom, chemists today say, the donating atom is being oxidized. So even when it bonds with carbon, hydrogen is being oxidized. Whenever an atom accepts electrons, chemists say it is being *reduced* because it is becoming more negatively charged. Oxidation and reduction are the two basic processes that take place in chemical reactions.

The number of electrons an atom donates to another atom is called its *oxidation state*. Hydrogen, for instance, has an oxidation state of +1 in compounds because it donates one electron. The oxidation number is the same as the electrical charge the hydrogen atom acquires when it bonds. Carbon has an oxidation state of +4 in carbon dioxide because it donates four electrons, but when carbon accepts electrons, its oxidation state is −4. Oxygen has an oxidation state of −2 in just about every compound.

Why is oxygen's attraction for other elements so strong? It seems it is so close to having a complete outer family that it never stops looking for two more electrons. Unlike carbon, oxygen never donates electrons because it has too many electrons in its outer family to give away to other families. It focuses just on getting electrons.

You might expect the element with one more electron than oxygen to have a greater attraction for other elements, since it is even closer to completing its outer family. Fluorine, with nine protons and electrons, is indeed more electronegative than oxygen. But chemists did not discover it until 1886; it bonds so strongly with other elements that they had difficulty separating it from its compounds!

Periodic Table

+1								
1 **H** 1.00794 Hydrogen								

+2 —— OXIDATION STATE

3 **Li** 6.941 Lithium	4 **Be** 9.01218 Beryllium							
11 **Na** 22.98977 Sodium	12 **Mg** 24.305 Magnesium							
19 **K** 39.0983 Potassium	20 **Ca** 40.078 Calcium	21 **Sc** 44.95591 Scandium	22 **Ti** 47.88 Titanium	23 **V** 50.9415 Vanadium	24 **Cr** 51.9161 Chromium	25 **Mn** 54.93805 Manganese	26 **Fe** 55.847 Iron	27 **Co** 58.9332 Cobalt
37 **Rb** 85.4678 Rubidium	38 **Sr** 87.62 Strontium	39 **Y** 88.9059 Yttrium	40 **Zr** 91.224 Zirconium	41 **Nb** 92.9064 Niobium	42 **Mo** 95.94 Molybdenum	43 **Tc** (98) Technetium	44 **Ru** 101.07 Ruthenium	45 **Rh** 102.9055 Rhodium
55 **Cs** 132.9054 Cesium	56 **Ba** 137.327 Barium	57 **La** * 138.9055 Lanthanum	72 **Hf** 178.49 Hafnium	73 **Ta** 180.9479 Tantalum	74 **W** 183.85 Tungsten	75 **Re** 186.207 Rhenium	76 **Os** 190.2 Osmium	77 **Ir** 192.22 Iridium
87 **Fr** (223) Francium	88 **Ra** 226.025 Radium	89 **Ac** ***** (227) Actinium	104 **Unq** (261)† (Unnilquadium)	105 **Unp** (262)† (Unnilpentium)	106 **Unh** (263)† (Unnilhoxium)	107 **Uns** (262)† (Unnilseptium)	108 **Uno** (265)† (Unniloctium)	109 **Une** (266)† (Unnilnonium)

Oxygen has 8 protons and electrons, so its atomic number is 8. In the periodic table, the elements line up in columns according to their primary oxidation state, the number of electrons they usually donate when they bond with other atoms.

58 **Ce** 140.115 Cerium	59 **Pr** 140.9077 Praseodymium	60 **Nd** 144.24 Neodymium	61 **Pm** (145) Promethium	62 **Sm** 150.36 Samarium
90 **Th** 232.0381 Thorium	91 **Pa** 231.0359 Protactinium	92 **U** 238.029 Uranium	93 **Np** 237.048 Neptunium	94 **Pu** (244) Plutonium

of the Elements

CHEMICAL SYMBOL   ATOMIC NUMBER

					0
+3	±4	-3	-2	-1	**2** **He** 4.00260 Helium
5 **B** 10.811 Boron	**6** **C** 12.011 Carbon	**7** **N** 14.067 Nitrogen	**8** **O** 15.994 Oxygen	**9** **F** 18.998403 Florine	**10** **Ne** 20.1797 Neon
13 **Al** 26.96154 Aluminum	**14** **Si** 28.0855 Silicon	**15** **P** 30.973762 Phosphorous	**16** **S** 32.066 Sulfur	**17** **Cl** 35.4527 Chlorine	**18** **Ar** 39.948 Argon

ATOMIC WEIGHT
ELEMENT NAME

28 **Ni** 58.693 Nickel	**29** **Cu** 63.546 copper	**30** **Zn** 65.39 Zinc	**31** **Ga** 69.723 Gallium	**32** **Ge** 72.61 Germanium	**33** **As** 72.9216 Arsenic	**34** **Se** 78.96 Selenium	**35** **Br** 79.904 Bromine	**36** **Kr** 83.80 Krypton
46 **Pd** 106.42 Palladium	**47** **Ag** 107.8682 Silver	**48** **Cd** 112.41 Cadmium	**49** **In** 114.82 Indium	**50** **Sn** 118.71 Tin	**51** **Sb** 121.757 Antimony	**52** **Te** 127.60 Tellurium	**53** **I** 126.9045 Iodine	**54** **Xe** 131.29 Xenon
78 **Pt** 195.08 Platinum	**79** **Au** 196.9665 Gold	**80** **Hg** 200.59 Mercury	**81** **Ti** 204.383 Thallium	**82** **Pb** 207.2 Lead	**83** **Bi** 208.9804 Bismuth	**84** **Po** (209) Polonium	**85** **At** (210) Astatine	**86** **Rn** (222) Radon

63 **Eu** 151.965 Europium	**64** **Gd** 157.25 Gadolinium	**65** **Tb** 158.9253 Terbium	**66** **Dy** 162.50 Dysprosium	**67** **Ho** 164.9303 Holmium	**68** **Er** 167.26 Erbium	**69** **Tm** 168.9342 Thulium	**70** **Yb** 173.04 Ytterbium	**71** **Lu** 174.967 Lutetium
95 **Am** (243) Americium	**96** **Cm** (247) Berkelium	**97** **Bk** (247) Berkelium	**98** **Cf** (251) Californium	**99** **Es** (252) Einsteinium	**100** **Fm** (257) Fermium	**101** **Md** (258) Mendelevium	**102** **No** (259) Nobelium	**103** **Lr** (260) Lawrencium

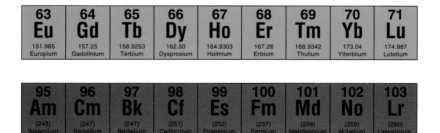

Fluorine is so reactive that an explosion takes place when it bonds with other elements. The same sometimes happens with oxygen. Hydrogen and oxygen, for instance, can explode when they form water if a spark is present. Whenever atoms bond, they give off heat, as if to express their joy over combining into one big family. Some elements, it seems, become so excited that an explosion takes place.

An explosion is simply the release of a tremendous amount of heat in a very short time. Fire is less extreme than an explosion. It ignites when the amount of heat generated by bonding atoms is too great to escape into the air slowly and invisibly like heat from a radiator. The intense heat flares into fire and light.

Usually, the atoms must be warmed slightly to encourage them to bond. When you strike a match, you are warming the carbon atoms in the match.

The more opposite in electronegativity two atoms are, the more chance fire will ignite when they bond. That is why oxygen is associated with fire. Chemists have discovered that one other element, chlorine, is also capable of generating fire when it bonds with certain elements. This green gas has seven outer electrons, like fluorine, except they are in the third, instead of the second, family.

The fire we see every day is an expression of oxygen's happiness over being united with other atoms. Oxygen's desire for bonding might be thought of as a burning passion, or love, for other elements. It is no wonder that people sometimes call a boyfriend or a girlfriend a "flame," and that it is considered romantic to sit in front of a fire.

FANNING THE FIRE

People have used the heat generated by oxygen in many ways. As long ago as 1782, Lavoisier found that if burning charcoal was fed a stream of pure oxygen, it got hot enough to melt a metal called platinum. This metal was so strong that no one had ever found a way to melt it before.

Today oxygen is very important in industry for both welding and cutting steel. In welding torches, oxygen is mixed with a fuel called acetylene so that it will burn at a very high temperature. The torch's flame heats up the metal and melts it, joining it to another piece of steel.

In cutting torches, a small flame heats up the metal, and then a great stream of oxygen gas flows onto it to do the actual cutting. The oxygen reacts with some of the iron, generating more heat to quickly melt the metal.

Oxygen is also used in making steel, which is a mixture of iron with carbon and other strengthening elements. Iron must be heated to high temperatures to make steel, and oxygen is fed into the furnace to make the fire hotter. Oxygen is also mixed with the fuel that propels massive rockets into space.

Although oxygen does many wonderful things in our world, its extreme reactivity can cause problems. In the air, it reacts with just about anything it comes into contact with. It does not create fire, but oxygen slowly oxidizes substances, particularly metals. The reddish rust on iron is just one example. By reacting with iron, oxygen steadily eats it away, a process called *corrosion*.

Oxygen eats away at metals by forming rust
and other oxides in corrosion.

Oxygen corrodes other metals in the same way. It turns copper green and turns silver and other metals black. So you see, the fire-breathing dragon can be destructive, too.

With the help of water, oxygen also causes wood and other *organic matter*—material from living things—to decay. But this is a benefit, because the dead matter shrinks and its nutrients become available to new plants.

Believe it or not, the same process takes place in our own bodies, as you will learn in the next chapter.

Chapter 5

THE FIRE OF LIFE

From the time Lavoisier began working with oxygen, he was fascinated by its effect on breathing, or *respiration*. Previously, he had thought that the purpose of air in respiration was simply to inflate the lungs like balloons. But after getting to know oxygen and the part it plays in combustion, he realized that oxygen taken in during breathing actually reacts chemically with substances in the body!

Lavoisier knew that animals exhale carbon dioxide and that when food and other organic materials are burned, they too release carbon dioxide. Organic substances are made mostly of carbon. Perhaps, he guessed, carbon from food in the body combines with inhaled oxy-

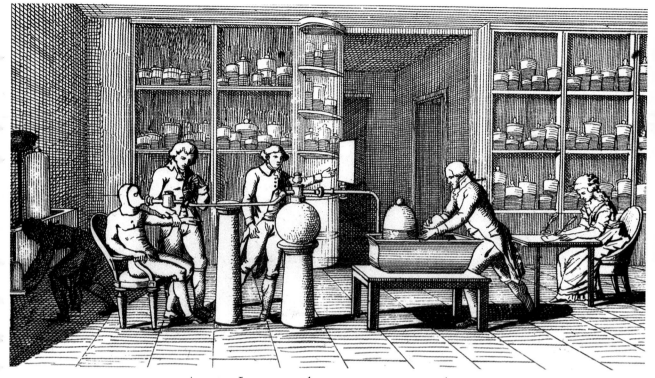

*Antoine Lavoisier, shown at center, carried out
experiments on human respiration.*

gen in a slow form of combustion. This chemical reaction
might be responsible for generating the heat in the body.

To find out whether his guess was correct, Lavoisier
did some tests with a guinea pig. He measured the amount
of carbon dioxide and heat the guinea pig gave off over a
period of time. He found that the amount of carbon dioxide was too small to account for all the heat generated.

Lavoisier eventually realized that the extra heat came from the bonding of oxygen with hydrogen in the food. In other words, both carbon and hydrogen are slowly burned in the body as a result of respiration. Lavoisier's experiment became famous, and people began calling anyone who's being used to test a new idea a guinea pig!

Lavoisier guessed that the combustion of hydrogen and carbon takes place in either the lungs or the blood. He knew that blood becomes bright red as it passes the lungs, just as iron and other metals turn red when they combine with oxygen. So he suspected that a metallic substance in the blood turns red when it encounters oxygen.

CELL FURNACES

Gradually, scientists learned that the lungs merely pass oxygen into the blood and that Lavoisier was right about the blood containing metal. Blood is blue when it arrives at the lungs, but turns red as oxygen attaches to iron in blood cells. The iron is inside a molecule of protein called *hemoglobin*. Each molecule of hemoglobin can carry four molecules of oxygen to cells throughout the body.

Body cells take food, as well as the oxygen, from the blood. Some of the foods are *carbohydrates*, which contain carbon and hydrogen. The cells oxidize the carbohydrates, producing carbon dioxide and water. As you know, this reaction produces energy, which the body needs to live. Thus, the slow fire burns in every cell of the body as

A molecule of hemoglobin inside a red blood cell contains iron atoms, shown in gray in this computer model.

part of a process called *metabolism*. The blood takes the carbon dioxide to the lungs to be exhaled, and the water is eliminated in sweat and urine.

Fortunately, the reverse process occurs in plants. They absorb the carbon dioxide that animals exhale, and they draw in water from the ground and air. Then energy from the sun breaks the bonds between carbon and oxygen and between hydrogen and oxygen. This process is called *photosynthesis*. The carbon and hydrogen bond to form carbohydrates, which the plants use to build more stems and leaves. The plants then release the oxygen into the air, which people and animals breathe.

Just as the oxidation of metals causes damage, oxidation in the body can be harmful, too. During metabolism,

Algae releases bubbles of oxygen into water. Like all plants, it absorbs carbon dioxide and gives off oxygen.

dangerous substances called *free radicals* sometimes form. These free radicals are molecules containing atoms that have a homeless electron or two. The electrons are so desperate to join the family of another atom that a free radical will bond with just about anything. In so doing, they can damage the immune system and mutate genes. Some people believe that a lot of free radicals in the body can lead to cancer.

Nutritionists recommend eating foods called *antioxidants* to stop the oxidizing process that leads to free radicals. Some antioxidants are vitamin C, vitamin E, and *beta-carotene*, all of which are found in fruits and vegetables.

OXYGEN IN OUR WORLD

In spite of free radicals, oxygen's effect on the body is overwhelmingly beneficial. In hospitals, patients with respiratory problems, such as emphysema and pneumonia, are put into oxygen tents to help them breathe. Oxygen can also enhance the effects of radiation therapy on patients with cancer.

But if healthy people breathe pure oxygen for too long, their lungs can become damaged. Lungs are designed for air that is only one-fifth oxygen. If we lived billions of years ago, we'd be in trouble. Long before animals appeared on earth, the atmosphere was mostly carbon dioxide. Gradually, enough oxygen was released from plants to bring it to its present level in the air.

Oxygen makes up almost half of the earth's crust, where it is found mostly in compounds. Sand, dirt, and other rocky material are oxides. Taking into consideration land, water, and air, oxygen forms about half of our world.

Most of the oxygen in the air is in the form of the gas O_2. But high up in the atmosphere, this gas is converted into a different form of oxygen called *ozone*. Light from the sun breaks apart the oxygen molecules, and each oxygen atom bonds to a nearby molecule to form O_3, a blue gas. Chemists call ozone an *allotrope* of oxygen.

Only a small part of the sun's light has enough energy to break apart O_2 molecules. This is called ultraviolet light, and it is invisible to us. The layer of ozone in the upper atmosphere absorbs ultraviolet light and keeps too much of it from reaching earth. Ultraviolet light causes sunburn if we stay in the sun for too long. If the burns are very severe or happen a lot, people can get skin cancer. Ultraviolet light can also damage immune systems and the cells of plants.

Ozone is even more reactive than O_2. The extra oxygen atom is always ready to combine with just about any other substance. Environmentalists worry that chemicals in spray cans and from farms and industries may be rising into the atmosphere and reacting with ozone. They believe the chemicals are causing a huge hole in the ozone layer over the South Pole. If people don't stop using them, environmentalists warn, the hole will get bigger and skin cancer will increase.

Ozone is a form of oxygen with three atoms in each molecule.

In 1992 the United States and other countries that use most of these chemicals agreed to gradually replace them by the year 2010 with other substances that do not harm the ozone layer.

Much as it does in the upper atmosphere, ultraviolet light can cause ozone to form near the earth's surface in very tiny amounts. In smog, polluting chemicals react

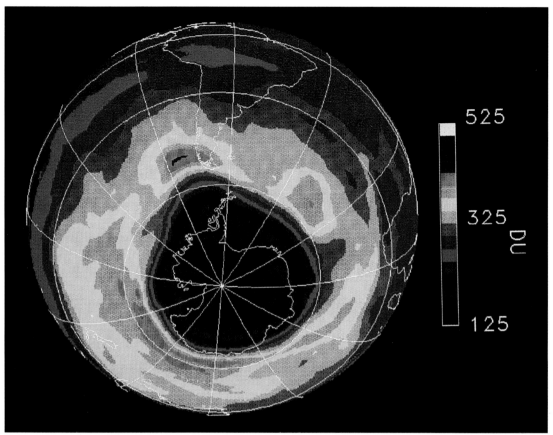

*This satellite map shows the hole (in black and purple)
in the ozone layer over Antarctica.*

with ultraviolet light to form more ozone. In significant
amounts, ozone is poisonous; it is so reactive that it
attacks tissues in the throat and lungs. When the amount
of ozone becomes too high, some cities issue an ozone
alert to warn people to stay inside.

So, hard as it is to believe, the life-giving gas we breathe can become destructive if one more oxygen atom is added to its molecule. Like a fire-breathing dragon, oxygen can be harmful at times, even though it has many wondrous qualities. It can bring warmth, light, life, and excitement—if you are careful that you don't get burned.

Oxygen is the element we know most intimately. It comes into our bodies every few seconds and rejuvenates us. Like a faithful friend, oxygen asks nothing in return. And as if that weren't enough, it has given us many of the things that make life worth living—fire, civilization, and perhaps even love!

Glossary

acetylene—an invisible gas that is burned as fuel.

acid—a chemical with a sour taste that can be neutralized by a group of chemicals called bases. Some acids are so powerful that they can eat through metals.

alchemist—a person who experimented with chemicals in the Middle Ages in order to find a way to change lead or other metals into gold. Many alchemists also sought spiritual growth and a cure for diseases.

allotrope—a form of an element that comes about because of the arrangment of its atoms in a molecule or a crystal. Ozone is an allotrope of oxygen.

antioxidant—a substance that prevents the oxidation of other substances.

atom—a tiny particle that is the smallest piece of an element.

Each element has an atom with a unique number of protons and electrons.

beta-carotene—a substance found in dark green and orange vegetables and fruits. It acts as an antioxidant in the body.

carbohydrates—substances in food that are compounds of mostly carbon and hydrogen.

carbon—an element with six protons and electrons. Charcoal is one form of carbon.

carbon dioxide—a gas that animals exhale and plants absorb. It is a compound of carbon and oxygen.

chemical reaction—a process in which substances combine or decompose to form new substances. In a chemical reaction, atoms bond together to form compounds or break apart into elements.

compound—a substance made up of two or more elements chemically bonded together.

corrosion—a process in which metals wear away because of a chemical reaction with oxygen and water.

earth—a term used before the nineteenth century to refer to the powdery substance produced when a metal burns in air. It arose from the four-element theory, in which earth was believed to be an element.

electron—a tiny particle that moves around the nucleus of an atom. It has a negative charge.

electronegative—having a tendency to attract electrons. Electronegative elements usually become negatively charged when they bond with other elements.

element—a basic substance that cannot be broken down into any simpler substance. There are 92 elements in nature, and almost 20 more have been generated artificially.

fire air—an eighteenth-century term for oxygen.

fixed air—an eighteenth-century term for carbon dioxide gas.

fluorine—a pale yellow gas that is the most electronegative of all the elements. With nine protons and electrons, fluorine is so reactive that it explodes when it bonds.

foul air—an eighteenth-century term for nitrogen.

free radical—a highly reactive atom or a group of bonded atoms with one or more electrons available for bonding.

gas—a substance that has no definite shape or volume, but spreads into whatever space is available. It is the form a substance takes when the temperature of its liquid form is raised so high that its molecules rise into the air.

hemoglobin—a protein in the blood that transports oxygen throughout the body.

hydrogen—the lightest of all the elements in weight. It is an invisible gas that burns in oxygen to produce water.

inflammable air—an eighteenth-century term for hydrogen.

lead oxide—a compound of lead and oxygen.

matter—anything that takes up space and has mass.

mercury—a silver liquid metal that is used in thermometers. It is an element with eighty protons and electrons.

metabolism—the process of digesting food and supplying energy to the body.

molecule—a group of two or more atoms bonded together to form a compound. They sometimes form in elements, too, especially gases.

nitrogen—an invisible gas that accounts for about four-fifths of the air. It is an element with seven protons and electrons.

nucleus—the center of an atom, where the protons and neutrons are located.

ore—a mineral, or a rocky material that contains a metal or some other valuable substance.

organic matter—material that comes from living things. It is made mostly of carbon and hydrogen.

oxidation state—the electrical charge that an atom acquires as a result of donating to or accepting electrons from another atom during bonding.

oxidize—to bond with oxygen, or, in general, to remove electrons from an atom through chemical bonding.

ozone—a blue gas containing three atoms of oxygen in its molecule. It is found in the upper atmosphere, in smog, and in bleaches and disinfectants.

phlogiston—an invisible substance that chemists in the eighteenth century believed caused fire. It does not really exist.

photosynthesis—the chemical process that takes place in plants. Carbon dioxide and water are changed into carbohydrates with the help of sunlight.

property—a quality or behavior that a substance displays.

proton—a particle in the center, or nucleus, of an atom with a positive electric charge. The number of protons in an atom determines which element it is.

reduce—to add electrons to an atom through chemical bonding.

respiration—the process through which oxygen is inhaled and supplied to the body and carbon dioxide is retrieved and exhaled.

ultraviolet light—an invisible portion of the sun's light that is more energetic than violet light. If skin is exposed to ultraviolet light for too long, it can burn.

Sources

Brock, William H. *The Norton History of Chemistry.* New York: W. W. Norton & Company, 1992.

Dictionary of Scientific Biography. New York: Scribner, 1970–80.

Farber, Eduard, ed. *Great Chemists.* New York: Interscience, 1961.

Hudson, John. *The History of Chemistry.* New York: Routledge, Chapman, & Hall, 1992.

Jaffe, Bernard. *Crucibles: The Story of Chemistry from Ancient Alchemy to Nuclear Fission.* New York: Simon & Schuster, 1948.

Newton, David E. *The Chemical Elements.* New York: Franklin Watts, 1994.

Partington, J. R. *A History of Chemistry.* London: Macmillan & Co., 1962.

Weeks, Mary Elvira. *Discovery of the Elements.* Easton, Penn.: Journal of Chemical Education, 1968.

Weibel, Ewald R. *The Pathway for Oxygen: Structure and Function in the Mammalian Respiratory System.* Cambridge, Mass.: Harvard University Press, 1984.

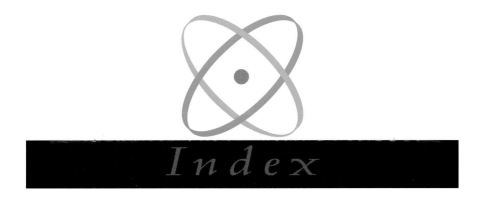

Index

Italicized numbers indicate illustrations.

Acetylene, 43

Acids, 14, 21

Air, 5, 7, 11–24, *18*, *20*, 25, 27, 32, 33, 34, 43, 50, 51

Alchemists, 12–15, *14*, 21–22, 29

Algae, *50*

Allotropes, 52

Antarctica, *54*

Antioxidants, 51

Atmosphere, the, 51–52

Atomic numbers, *40–41*

Atoms, 33, 34, *34*, 35, 36, 37, *37*, 38, 42, 51, 52, *53*, 55

Atoms, paired, 34

Betacarotene, 51

Black, Joseph, 21

Blood, *8*, 17, 48, 49, *49*

Bonding, 8, 35, 36–45, *37*, *38*, 48, 52

Breathing, 7, 8, 16–17, *18*, 24, 46, 51. *See also* Respiration

Cancer, 51, 52

Carbohydrates, 48, 50

Carbon, 28, 38, 39, 43, 46, 48, 50

Carbon atoms, 38, *38*, 42

Carbon dioxide, 21, 25, 28, 34, 38, 39, 46, 47, 49, *50*, 51, 52

Carbon dioxide molecules, 38

Cavendish, Henry, 21, 28

Charcoal, 15, 21, 28, 43

Chemical reactions, 12, 14, 15, 28, 39, 47

Chemistry, 30

Chinese, ancient, 15

Chlorine, 42

Combustion, 27, 29, 47, 48. *See also* Explosions

Compounds, 28, 29, 30, 31, 32, 33, 35, 39, 52

Copper, 11, 45

Corrosion, 43, *44*, 45. *See also* Oxidation, Rust

Dalton, John, 32–33

da Vinci, Leonardo, 16–17, *16*

Electricity, 35–36

Electronegativity, 35–36, 38, 39, 42

Electrons, 36, 37, 38, 39, 42, 51

Elements, 12, 29–30, 31, 33, 35, 36–37. *See also* Four Elements, theory of

Empedocles, 11–12

Emphysema, 51

Explosions, 42. *See also* Combustion

Fire, 5–7, *6*, 8, 9–11, *10*, 12, 14, 15–19, 21, 22–23, 24, 25–28, 29, 30, 42, 43–45, 48, 55

Fire air, 23, 27

Fixed air, 21

Foul air, 23

Four elements, theory of, 12, *13*, 16, 17, 29

Free radicals, 51

Fluorine, 39–42

Gases, 22, 28, 31, 32, 33, 34, 35, 42, 52, 55

Genes, 51

Gold, 12, 29

Greeks, ancient, 11–12

Hales, Stephen, 19–21

Hemoglobin, 48

Hemoglobin molecules, *49*

Hydrogen, 21, 27–29, 33, 34, 35, 38, 39, 42, 48, 50

Hydrogen atoms, 37, *37*, 38

Immune system, the, 51, 52

"Inflammable air," 21, 27

Iron, 11, 15, 29, 43, 48, *49*

Lavoisier, Antoine, 27, 28, 29, *30*, 31, 35, 43, 46, *47*, 48

Lead, 11, 12, 14, 20, 21, 24, 29, 30

Lead oxide, 30

Lungs, 7, 17, 48, 49, 51, 54

Mao-Khóa, 15–16

Matter, 12

Mayow, John, 17–19

Mercuric oxide, 30

Mercury, 23–24, *26*, 30

Metabolism, 49, 50

Metals, 11, 12, 14, 15, 19, 21, 24, 25, 26, 29, 43, 48, 50

Molecules, 33, 34, *34*, 38, 48, *49*, 52, *53*, 55

Negative electrical charges, 35, 36, 38, 39

Nitrogen, 15, 23, 25, 27, 32, 33, 34

Nucleus, 36, 37

Ore, 11

Organic matter, 45, 46

Oxidation number, 39

Oxidation state, 39

Oxides, 30, 52

Oxidation, 36, 39, 48, 51. *See also* Corrosion, Rust

Oxygen, liquid, 32
Oxygen atoms, 34, 34, 36, 37, 38, 52, 55
Oxygen molecules, 52, 55
Oxygen tents, 51
Ozone, 52–55, 53
Ozone layer, the, 52–53, 54

Periodic table, 40–41
Phlogiston, 19, 25, 26, 28, 29
Photosynthesis, 50, 52
Plants, 8, 21, 25, 45, 51
Platinum, 43
Pneumonia, 51
Pollution, 52–55
Positive electrical charges, 35, 38
Priestley, Joseph, 23–24, 23, 25, 29
Proteins, 48
Protons, 36, 39

Radiation therapy, 51
Reduction, 39
Respiration, 46–49, 51, 55. *See also* Breathing
Respiratory problems, 51
Rocket fuel, 43

Rust, 15, 36, 43, 44. *See also* Corrosion, Oxidation

Scheele, Carl William, 22–23, 22, 25, 29
Silver, 11, 29, 45
Skin cancer, 52
Smog, 53
South Pole, 52
Steel, 43
Steel, cutting, 43
Sweat, 49

Ultraviolet light, 52–54
United States, 53
Urine, 49

Vitamin C, 51
Vitamin E, 51

Water, 11, 12, 18, 19, 20, 27–29, 33, 34, 35, 37, 42, 45, 48, 49, 50
Water vapor, 32, 33
Welding, 43

Yang, 15
Yin, 15

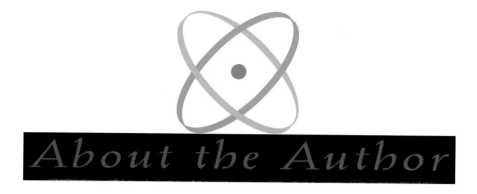

About the Author

Karen Fitzgerald is a science writer and an editor with Franklin Watts. She has worked as an editor for *The Sciences,* a magazine published by the New York Academy of Sciences, and *Spectrum,* a technology magazine published by the Institute of Electrical and Electronics Engineers. She has written articles for magazines including *Scientific American, Omni,* and *Science World.* Her bachelor's degree is in mechanical engineering from the University of Illinois in Urbana, and she has a master's degree in science and environmental reporting from New York University.